God Is Here, I'm Not Afraid

By Evelyn Amuedo Wade
Illustrated by Kathy Rogers

Augsburg • *Minneapolis*

GOD IS HERE, I'M NOT AFRAID

Text copyright © 1988 Evelyn Amuedo Wade
Copyright © 1988 Augsburg Fortress

All rights reserved. Except for brief quotations in critical articles and reviews, no part of this book may be reproduced in any manner without prior written permission from the publisher. Write to: Permissions, Augsburg Fortress, 426 S. Fifth St., Box 1209, Minneapolis MN 55440.

ISBN 0-8066-2382-9   LCCN 88-83019

Manufactured in the U.S.A.   AF 10-2646

1 2 3 4 5 6 7 8 9 0 1 2 3 4 5 6 7 8 9

To Lillie, Rebecca, and Cullen,
who have added a whole new glow to my life,
this book is joyfully dedicated.

"Don't be afraid, Rebecca," I tell my baby sister
when there's a storm about to break.
"God made the storm."
I smile at her and let her hold my hand.

But she's so young. She doesn't know as yet—
she doesn't understand that God is everywhere,
and God takes care of kids like us.

Sometimes she makes a fuss because the wind is strong and whistles through the trees, and leaves go swirling through the air, and all the branches bend like giants on their knees. And garbage cans go crashing down the street.

Papers swirl and sparrows fly away. But I remind Rebecca, "Don't be afraid, 'cause God is here, and God is everywhere."

"God's in the wind and in the trees and in the bushes by the street," my little brother Joey says. "I like a storm. I think it's neat."

And then he smiles and squares his shoulders. "I'm not afraid," he says. "I used to be, but then I prayed. And do you know what? God helped me to be brave."

"God always helps," I say. "All you have to do
is ask. You see, Rebecca, God made the wind,
and do you know why? So we'd have breezes
in the summer, and so boats could sail and
seeds could blow about and all the washing on
the line could dry.

"God made the trees so we'd have wood, and
birds could have a place to build their nests.
And when the branches bend, it's just as if the
trees are bowing to our Lord. Remember,
everything God made is good."

Then, just before the rain comes down, and all the light
begins to fade, Rebecca hides her eyes and says, "I'm still afraid.
I just don't like it when everything is dark and cold.
I like it when the sky is blue and clouds are white and flowers
wink their eyes at me and everything is bright
and all the world is painted gold with sunshine.
I hate the dark."

But Joey pats her hand and says, "It's all right, Becky.
God made the dark. God sees right through the cloudy sky
to take good care of you."

And then the thunder rolls—a rumbling, grumbling, bumbling kind of sound
—and Rebecca holds her ears and cries, "I'm scared, I'm scared!"
with eyes as round and dark as empty flowerpots.

We stop to listen then, the three of us, and over there beyond the hill
there's lots of rumbling from the sky, just like the sound
when Grandma drops a cookie sheet.

"God made the thunder," Joey says. "And when it comes,
it makes me wonder if a million soldiers beating on their drums
are marching up the hill."

"God made all the noises that you hear, and all the things you see,"
I tell them both. (I know these things 'cause I'm the oldest one of all.)

But then the lightning strikes. It streaks across the sky and lights up all the world as if a hundred candles had been lit to chase the dark away.

I *like* to watch the lightning, sitting here inside where everything is warm and dry. But Rebecca wants to hide.

So I remind her, "Don't cry, Rebecca. God made the lightning. It clears the air. And later when the rain is gone, we'll go outside to play in air as fresh as morning dew."

"*I* understand," my brother says. "And do you know what? God made the dew. God made me, Becky, and God made you. And everything God made is good."

And then, down comes the rain. It crashes against the windowpane and splashes puddles in the yard.

"Rain's not good," Rebecca says. "It makes the whole world squashy. It wets my hair and ruins all the washing on the line. And when it rains, we can't go out to play. I think the rain is mean."

"Rain makes the flowers grow," I say. "It feeds the plants so we'll have food. It makes the rivers flow, so cows and horses get enough to drink, and it washes the flowers and keeps the whole world clean. Rain is *good*."

But Rebecca shakes her head. "It makes me cry," she says.

"Rebecca, sometimes sad things happen. Remember how we cried
the day the puppy ran away? But God has reasons for the things
that happen—even if we don't know why. And sometimes
the things we fear are really God's way of showing us he's near.

"Do you know, Rebecca, that Jesus is the Son of God?
And God sent Jesus down to earth to care for kids like us,
to love us and to share God's many gifts with us."

"The flowers and the trees, the oceans and the lakes, the birds and bees, the sunshine and the stars, the thunder and the rain, the lightning and the wind—they all belong to God. And we do too."

"We're kids and we don't always know about the mysteries of outer space, why God makes things the way they are, why darkness comes at night and sunshine comes by day, why birds have wings, and breezes blow, and why it is that every star stays happy in its place. But we know that God loves us."

Then suddenly Rebecca smiles. She reaches
out her little arms and opens up her hands as
if to let the fear go dribbling through her
fingers.

"You see?" she says, "the scared is gone. God
took it all away. I prayed like Joey told me to,
and now I'm not afraid. God loves me. And I
love God."

And even though there's lightning in the sky,
and even though the thunder rolls,
Rebecca smiles, 'cause now she knows that God is here.
And God takes care of kids, no matter where they are.